About Mammals

About Mammals

A Guide for Children

Cathryn Sill

Illustrated by John Sill

PEACHTREE

ATLANTA

For the One who created mammals.

—*Genesis* 1:24

Published by
PEACHTREE PUBLISHERS, LTD.
494 Armour Circle NE
Atlanta, Georgia 30324

Jacket illustration by John Sill

Printed in Hong Kong

10 9 8 7 6 5 4 3 2 1
First Edition

Library of Congress Cataloging-in-Publication Data

Sill, Cathryn P.
   About mammals: a guide for children / Cathryn Sill; illustrated by John
Sill.—lst ed.
       p.   cm.
   Summary: Explains what mammals are, how they live, and what they do.
   ISBN 1-56145-141-X (hardcover)
   I. Mammals—Juvenile literature. [I. Mammals.] I. Sill, John, ill. II. Title.
   QL706.2.S547 1997
   500—dc20   96-36402
                                                          CIP
                                                          AC

About Mammals

Mammals have hair.

PLATE 1
Raccoon

John Sill

They may have thick fur,

sharp quills,

John Sill

or only a few stiff whiskers.

PLATE 4
Walrus

Baby mammals drink milk from their mothers.

PLATE 5
Bison

Some mammals are born helpless.

PLATE 6
White-footed Mice

Others can move about on their own
soon after they are born.

Mammals may run,

PLATE 8
Pronghorns

climb,

PLATE 9
Red Squirrel

swim,

PLATE 10
Blue Whale

John Gill

or fly.

PLATE 11
Big Brown Bat

Mammals eat meat,

PLATE 12
Bobcat

plants,

PLATE 13
Pika

or both.

PLATE 14
Black Bear

They may live in cold, icy places...

hot, dry deserts…

PLATE 16
Blacktail Jackrabbit

or wet marshes.

PLATE 17
Muskrat

It is important to protect mammals where they live.

PLATE 18
Humans, Raccoon,
Gray Squirrel,
White-tailed Deer

Afterword

PLATE 1
Hair in its different forms protects mammals in ways uniquely adapted for each species. Raccoons are found in each of the lower forty-eight states.

PLATE 2
Musk Oxen live in the cold Arctic region. They have a thick outer coat of long guard hairs covering a dense undercoat that keeps them warm in frigid temperatures.

PLATE 3
Porcupines have sharp stiff quills on their backs and tails. The quills are loosely attached and will come off and stick into an enemy's body.

PLATE 4
Some marine mammals have only a few coarse whiskers. Walruses use their sensitive, bristly whiskers to forage for food on the ocean floor. They eat snails, clams, crabs, and shrimp.

PLATE 5

Bison, also called American Buffalo, were nearly hunted to extinction in the late 1800s. They are now protected and their numbers have slowly increased. Bison are the largest land animals in North America.

PLATE 6

White-footed Mice babies are weaned when they are about three weeks old.

PLATE 7

Baby Elk must be able to run very fast soon after birth to avoid danger from predators (animals that eat other animals). Newborn Elk can stand up about twenty minutes after birth.

PLATE 8

Pronghorns can run over fifty miles per hour for several miles. They are the fastest mammals in North America.

PLATE 9

Red Squirrels are small, noisy tree squirrels. Squirrels are rodents. Rodents' teeth continue to grow all their lives. These animals must gnaw a great deal of the time to keep their teeth worn down.

PLATE 10

Blue Whales are the largest animals in the world. They grow up to 100 feet and may weigh 200 tons.

PLATE 11

Bats are the only mammals that truly fly. Big Brown Bats have a body length of $4\frac{1}{8}$ to 5 inches. They can fly at speeds up to forty miles per hour. Bats are very beneficial because many of them feed on insects.

PLATE 12

Though Bobcats can kill animals larger than themselves, they hunt mainly rabbits, squirrels, and mice.

PLATE 13

In midsummer, Pikas begin to gather plants which they pile into stacks to dry in the sun. They store these haystacks for winter food. Pikas do not hibernate in winter, but move about in tunnels they dig.

PLATE 14

Black Bears are the most common bear in North America. They will eat many different things including roots, berries, insects, and small mammals.

PLATE 15

The white winter coats of Arctic Foxes change to brown in summer. This camouflage or protective coloration allows them to hide from both predators and prey.

PLATE 16

Blacktail Jackrabbits are not really rabbits, but hares. Hares do not dig burrows and their young are born fully furred with their eyes open. Jackrabbits have very keen hearing which helps them to avoid predators.

PLATE 17
Muskrats have a tail that is flattened from side to side. They use this flattened tail to guide them as they swim. Muskrats build their domed houses in water using marsh vegetation.

PLATE 18
One of the primary dangers to mammals is habitat destruction. We must be responsible to maintain an environment where mammals are provided space, shelter, food, and water.
Can you find the animal in this picture that is not a mammal?

Cathryn Sill is an elementary-school teacher in Franklin, North Carolina, and the author of ABOUT BIRDS, the first entry in the ABOUT… series. With her husband John and her brother-in-law Ben Sill, she co-authored the popular bird-guide parodies A FIELD GUIDE TO LITTLE KNOWN AND SELDOM-SEEN BIRDS OF NORTH AMERICA, ANOTHER FIELD GUIDE TO LITTLE KNOWN AND SELDOM-SEEN BIRDS OF NORTH AMERICA, and BEYOND BIRDWATCHING.

John Sill is a prize-winning and widely published wildlife artist who illustrated ABOUT BIRDS, and illustrated and co-authored the FIELD GUIDES and BEYOND BIRDWATCHING. A native of North Carolina, he holds a B.S. in Wildlife Biology from North Carolina State University.